If You Decide to Go to the moon

If You Decide to Go to the moon

By **FAITH MCNULTY**

Illustrated by **STEVEN KELLOGG**

SCHOLASTIC INC.

New York   Toronto   London   Auckland   Sydney
Mexico City   New Delhi   Hong Kong   Buenos Aires

If you decide to go to the moon
in your own rocket ship,
read this book before you start.

It will tell you how to get there
and what to do after you land.
The most important part tells
you how to get home.

Check the things you will need:
space suit, air tanks, books, and games.
Don't forget your diary and plenty of food.
Peanut butter, apples, and cake
will taste good in space.
Water and juice are also important.

To get to the moon, you will travel
about 240,000 miles—
a long trip, but rocket ships go fast.
If you average 3,750 miles per hour,
you will get there in two-and-a-half days.

Get aboard. Close the hatch. Light the burners.

TEN

NINE

EIGHT

SEVEN

SIX

FIVE

FOUR

THREE

TWO

ONE

BLAST OFF!

You shoot up . . . up . . . up into the sky.
As your ship rises through the clouds,
your body is pressed against the seat.
At first you feel very heavy. Don't worry.
This feeling will go away.

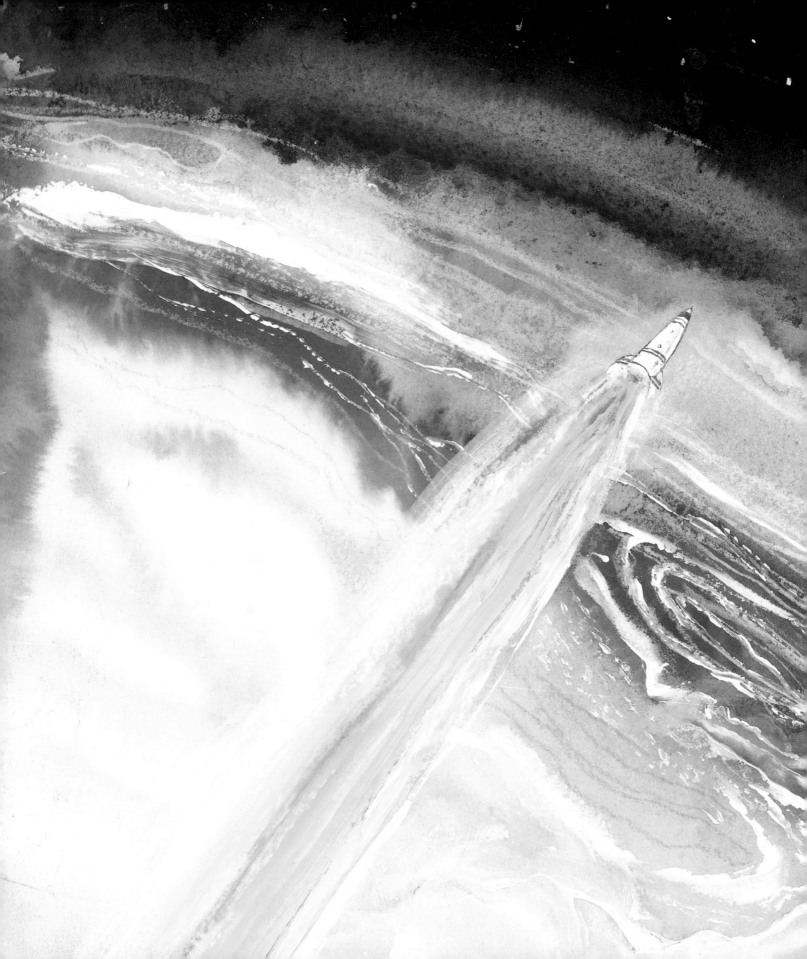

For a few seconds you fly
through a mixture of clouds and air
and dust that hangs over the earth.
It is not very thick—only about fifteen miles.
You will shoot right through it into space.

Space is dark and empty. . . .
There is no air in space; no clouds; no rain;
only a few specks of dust,
some rocks called meteors,
and some chunks of ice called comets.
Both meteors and comets are pieces of stars
that exploded long ago and have been
flying around in space ever since.
If one hit you, it would be very bad,
but space is so big and you are so small
that a collision is unlikely.
In the blackness of space
the stars shine like a million fireflies.

The sun blazes with fiery light,
and the moon, the mysterious moon,
glows like a pearl in the black, black sky.
Of course, you know that the moon
has no light of its own.
It glows in the light of the sun.

Up here in space
you may feel very alone.
Don't look back at the Earth.
It would make you even lonelier.
This is the time to play some cheerful music,
eat a peanut butter sandwich,
keep your eyes fixed on the shining moon,
and settle down for a long ride.

Relax. Take off your seat belt and
be prepared for a surprise.
Because you are weightless in space,
you'll feel amazingly light.
You will float like a feather
inside the cabin and bounce
off the cabin walls.
But you'll bounce very lightly
and find it a lot of fun.

When you are thirsty, don't try to pour
orange juice into a glass.
With everything weightless,
it would collect into floating liquid balls
and become an orange juice blob.
You can drink out of a squeeze bottle instead.
After supper and a squeeze of juice,
it's time for bed.

Tie yourself to your bunk so you won't float away,
and settle down for a good night's sleep.
Of course, there is no night in space.
You will have to pretend.
Try to have sweet dreams.

When you wake you will be much closer to the moon.
It will be big and round and very bright
with dark patches that look like lakes or seas.
They were made billions of years ago
when the moon was very hot,
hot enough to melt stone.

Now and then, melted stone
spurted up through the crust
and spread out on the surface
like spilled soup.
When it cooled, it hardened
into stone, called lava.
From Earth, these smooth,
dark places look like oceans.

Playing cards will help to pass the time,
but if you drop them they will drift
around the cabin like butterflies.
Floating around to catch them
feels like swimming in a dream.

The first humans to go to the moon
landed on the Sea of Tranquility.
It is marked on your moon map
and would be a good place to land.

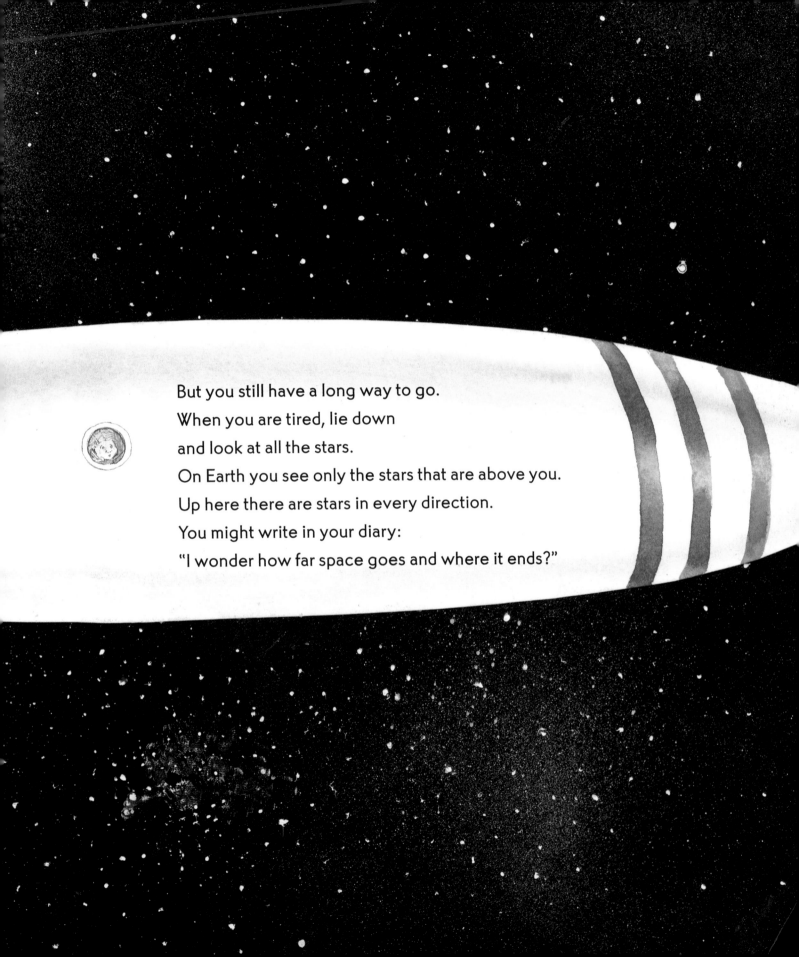

But you still have a long way to go.
When you are tired, lie down
and look at all the stars.
On Earth you see only the stars that are above you.
Up here there are stars in every direction.
You might write in your diary:
"I wonder how far space goes and where it ends?"

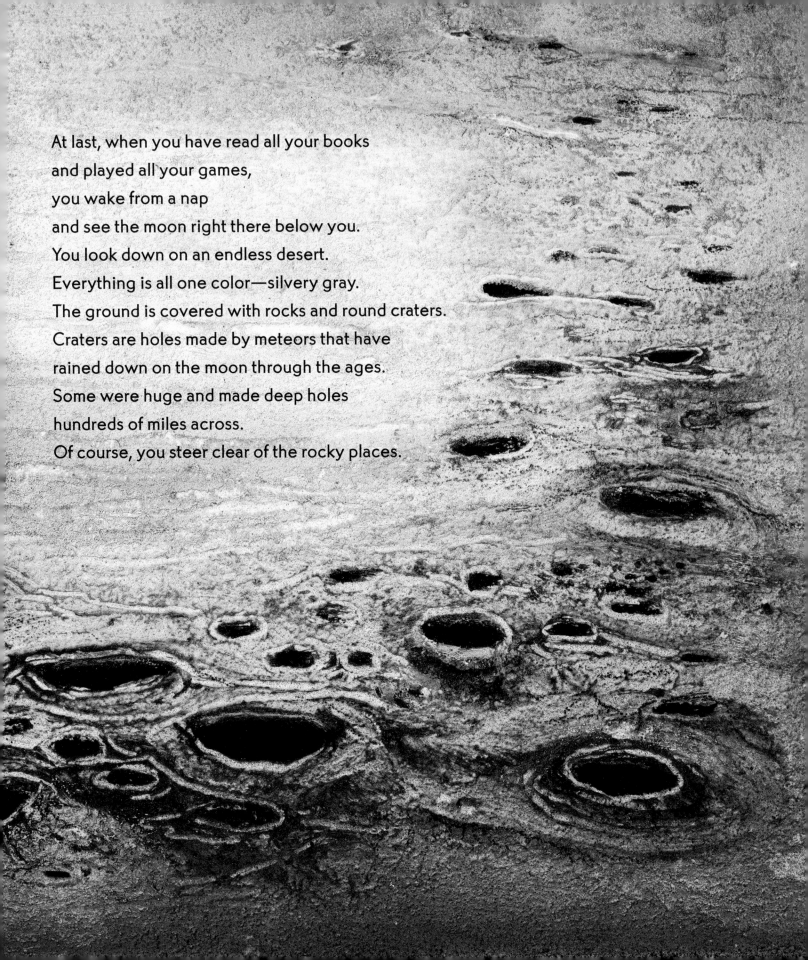

At last, when you have read all your books
and played all your games,
you wake from a nap
and see the moon right there below you.
You look down on an endless desert.
Everything is all one color—silvery gray.
The ground is covered with rocks and round craters.
Craters are holes made by meteors that have
rained down on the moon through the ages.
Some were huge and made deep holes
hundreds of miles across.
Of course, you steer clear of the rocky places.

At last you see
a lava lake below—
the Sea of Tranquility.
Get ready to land!
As you descend,
your craft shivers and shakes.
It settles softly.
You feel a bump.

YOU ARE ON THE MOON!

Your first look will be disappointing.
All you see through your porthole
is a cloud of dust stirred up by your landing.
Put on your space suit and air tank while
you wait for it to settle.
Then open the hatch and jump out.

You will land lightly.
The moon is smaller than
the Earth and has less gravity
to pull you down.
If you weigh sixty pounds on Earth,
you will weigh only ten on the moon.

Your first step will be difficult.
You will rise in the air and leap forward
like a kangaroo, but once you learn how,
walking will be fun.

Each step takes you five times as far
as a step on Earth.
Leaping over boulders and craters,
you cover the ground with magical swiftness.
The moonscape is strange,
but it doesn't look dangerous.
The dust reminds you of cake flour.
You wish you could take off your suit
and play in it.

DON'T DO IT!

The heat of the sun would burn you up!

Because there is no air or water on the moon,
there are no clouds to shield it from the heat
of the sun, or the cold of space.
Anything touched by the sun is blistering hot.
Anything in shadow is instantly cold.
Without a space suit, you would sizzle or freeze.

As you walk, you will notice that
your boots don't crunch on the pebbles.
If you take a hammer and hit a rock,
there is no bang.
It is impossible to make a noise on the moon.
Without air to carry sound waves,
you can't hear a bell ring, you can't hear a horn blow.
You can't hear a whistle or a song on the moon.
If you kick a pebble, it will bounce without a sound.

As you keep walking,
the silence and stillness are eerie.
Nothing moves.
The boulders and hills have strange shapes.
Some hills look like dinosaurs;
some boulders look like giant turtles,
or weird birds, or a herd of cows.
A heap of jagged rocks looks like a ruined castle.
You feel as if you might be in a fairy tale.
Or is it a dream?

Your map tells you that the
astronauts' camp is just over the next hill.
As you climb you wonder
if things will look different on the other side.
Will you find something green?
Something alive? A meadow of moongrass?
A herd of mooncows?

The answer is "no.

The hills stretch on and on
to the horizon, where the rim of the moon
meets the blackness of space.
Everything on the moon is lifeless and still.

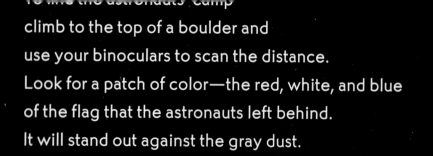

climb to the top of a boulder and
use your binoculars to scan the distance.
Look for a patch of color—the red, white, and blue
of the flag that the astronauts left behind.
It will stand out against the gray dust.

As you get close to the camp,
you will see everything the astronauts
left behind. Strewn amidst the lunar dust,
tools and equipment are scattered about.
Their boot prints look fresh,
as though they were made a moment ago.
There is no wind or rain to wear them away.
The astronauts left a message for
anyone who visits the moon.
You find it written on a plaque:
Here men from the planet Earth
first set foot on the moon. July 1969 A.D.

But the flag they planted isn't flying.
The flagpole was blown over from the blast
when the astronauts took off
and the flag is lying in the dust.
You pick it up and push it deep into the sand.
The flag is stiffened with wires so that it looks
as though it is flying even though there is no wind.
It is a brave and wonderful sight and reminds you
of the courage of the astronauts who brought it here.

If astronauts ever return
they will find the flag flying once again,
and your footprints in the dust.

By now your tank of air must be half empty.
It's time to return to your ship.
Your trail of footprints will lead you back.
You retrace your steps in leaps and bounds.
When you see your spaceship waiting,
you are suddenly terribly homesick.
You can't wait to get back to Earth. . . .
Take a last look at the moonscape.
Get aboard. Close the hatch
and pray that the computers will start.

You push buttons.
Lights flicker. Machinery whirs.
Rockets fire. Your ship lifts off.
Your heart lifts, too,
but you have thousands of miles
to travel. You'll just have to be patient.

You will see a beautiful sight—
Earth, surrounded by stars,
shining like a blue-and-white ball
on a Christmas tree.

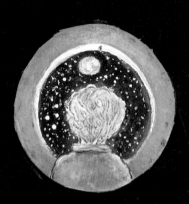

The nearer you get to Earth,
the more wonderful Earth will seem.
Finally, you are close enough to see
the continents and the oceans.
You can see clouds and rain and wind
moving across them, connecting
everything on Earth.

Your trip is almost over.
Your ship has reached the atmosphere.
You drop down through clouds
and land on green grass.

You jump out, thankful for
a miraculous journey and a safe return.

As you bend down to kiss the ground,
you promise you will always do your best
to protect all life on our beautiful Earth.

To Katherine White

—F. M.

To Bailey with love

—S. K.

Sincere thanks to Dr. Neil de Grasse Tyson, Director of the Hayden Planetarium, New York City

Earthlings in Space

Written by David Corke

Contents

Earthlings in Space is a report published in the year A.D. 3970 by the Interplanetary Council to commemorate more than 2,000 years of earthlings' travels in space. The report, as well as giving the latest information about recent discoveries in space, includes some historical background on the early earth colonies and their spread throughout the solar system.

Visions of the Future

Science-fiction writers include great visionaries whose dreams of the future often become the realities of today.

The first lunar landing that stirred the imagination of Robert Goddard, the "Father of Modern Rocketry," happened in *From the Earth to the Moon*, written in 1865 by Jules Verne. Even though Verne was a meticulous researcher and student of science, *real* scientists scoffed at the notion of space travel. All the facts pointed to one conclusion — space travel is impossible.

In 1969, three Americans, rocketed into outer space by Saturn V, landed on the moon. On that day, Wernher von Braun, the leader of the Saturn V project, realized his lifelong dream of space travel, which began at age twelve as he raced through the pages of a marvelous space adventure, *From the Earth to the Moon*.

Good science fiction is just what its name implies — a great story grounded in science. Nonfiction is often just a matter of time.

3

PART ONE

Earthlings in Space: A Report

Timeline of Events in the Report

Earth Year 2070 **Problems on Earth As the Years of Eco - terror Begin**
Earth's population reaches sixteen billion. Famines and environmental disasters, such as pollution of the atmosphere and rising seawater, affect most countries. Population starts to fall. Some mineral supplies are nearly exhausted.

Earth Year 2157 **Armstrong Base Established on Moon**
Colonization of the moon and establishment of exploratory bases to mine minerals on the moon become targets of the Interplanetary Council. Armstrong Base is established on the moon.

Earth Year 2212 **Space Station Island One Established**
Colonists at Armstrong complete the building of an earth-orbiting space station called Island One to launch expeditions to other planets.

Earth Year 2375 **Colonies on Mars Established**
Colonists establish first Mars base at Mariner A.

Earth Year 2783 **Colonies on Mercury Established**
Three colonies establish bases on Mercury to extract rare metals.

Earth Year 2956	**Work Begins on Venus — the Hostile Planet** Astronauts from Armstrong and Island One begin first stage of a two-stage program to alter the hostile environment of Venus.
Earth Year 3117	**Establishment of a Base on Ganymede** Colony established on Ganymede, a moon of Jupiter, to recover hydrogen from Jupiter.
Earth Year 3340	**Establishment of a Base on Titan** Exploration and research teams set up base on Titan, the largest of Saturn's moons.
Earth Year 3891	**New Planets Discovered** Astronomers at Titan base report sightings of planets at the distant Alpha Centauri star system. Radio signals also received from this region.
Earth Year 3933	**Starship *Daedalus* Is Launched: Destination Alpha Centauri** Starship *Daedalus* sets out on ninety-year round trip to Alpha Centauri.
Earth Year 3970	**Discovery of Icarus** Crew of *Daedalus* discovers and names Icarus, the first of several planets found orbiting the star system Alpha Centauri.

Earth Year 2070

Problems on Earth As the Years of Eco-terror Begin

The first environmental crisis reached its peak in Earth Year 2073. Mineral supplies were running out. Earth communities began to suffer from a series of environmental disasters. The greenhouse effect (caused by pollution from industrial gases) had raised the earth's temperature by 20°F. The Antarctic icecap began to melt, causing rising seas to flood cities and farmlands. Millions of people had nowhere to go. Many died from starvation, because acid rain destroyed forests and crops. Earth's population fell from 16 billion to 9.8 billion.

A second environmental crisis struck in Earth Year 2551. A large hole in the ozone layer allowed dangerous ultraviolet radiation to reach the ground, destroying crops and other vegetation. This loss of plant life caused the oxygen in the atmosphere to drop from around twenty percent to twelve percent, making it difficult for people to breathe. A series of worldwide famines gradually reduced the population from 15 billion to about 3.2 billion. This second age of "eco-terror" lasted for about one hundred and fifty years.

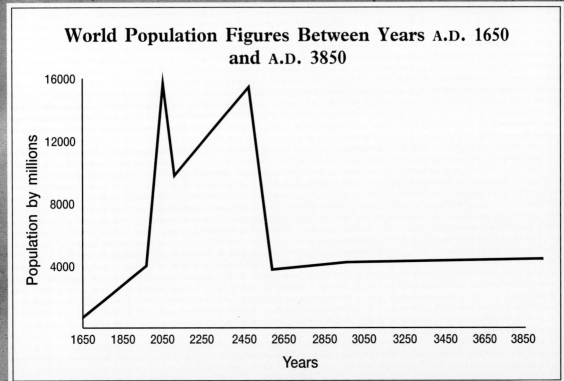

World Population Figures Between Years A.D. 1650 and A.D. 3850

Population by millions (y-axis): 4000, 8000, 12000, 16000

Years (x-axis): 1650, 1850, 2050, 2250, 2450, 2650, 2850, 3050, 3250, 3450, 3650, 3850

Earth Year 2157

Armstrong Base Established on Moon

The first environmental crisis of 2073 forced people to realize that industry and power generation had to be reduced if earth was to survive. Scientists began planning experiments to settle humans on nearby planets in the solar system, where industry and power generation could not harm living organisms.

In A.D. 2157, a small base was built on the moon. It was called the Armstrong Base (after the first astronaut to set foot on the moon in Earth Year 1969). Two hundred years later, this settlement had a large population of genetically engineered human beings called *mutants*. These mutants had their bodies changed so that they could live more easily in an environment so different from earth's. Most of these mutants were scientists and astronauts. Their tasks were to organize the building of space station Island One, to set out plans for new colonies on the nearby planets, and to send exploration teams to the moons of Jupiter and Saturn.

The Moon: Site of the Armstrong Base

The moon is earth's nearest neighbor. It is 239,000 miles from earth. Surface temperatures range from a minimum of −280°F to a maximum of 230°F. A lunar day is 336 hours long. The moon has one-sixth the gravity of earth. A 120-pound person would weigh only about 20 pounds and could jump to a height of about forty-five feet!

Today, in Earth Year 3970

There are 350,000 people at Armstrong Base.

Humans living and working on the moon still have to face the following problems:

- The moon has no atmosphere to absorb X rays, gamma rays, ultraviolet radiation, or meteorite impacts. Even very small meteors do great damage.
- Astronauts still need to supply all their oxygen, water, and food.
- All communication has to be made by radio. There is no air to carry sound waves.
- Astronauts have to depend mostly on nuclear fusion for energy. There are no oil supplies on the moon, but there is constant solar radiation for fourteen Earth days at a time. During this time solar energy can be used.

Earth Year 2212

Space Station Island One Established

By Earth Year 2212, the colonists at Armstrong had built a large space station called Island One.

At the center of Island One, colonists built a zero-gravity launching platform. Spacecraft launched from Island One did not need to reach high speeds to escape the gravitational attraction of the space station. These low-energy launchings were one of the main advantages of Island One in the space exploration program.

Earthlings on Island One grew all the food they needed in greenhouse gardens. Genetically engineered plants grew rapidly in the continuous sunlight. The most difficult problem was the supply of water. Water had to be made by combining oxygen (produced by tropical plants grown in large greenhouses) and hydrogen.

Safety and Life Support on Space Stations

Earthlings living on space stations need to be protected from many stresses and dangers that are not found on earth.

Pressure   On earth, we live under a constant pressure from the air in the atmosphere. Without this pressure our bodies would explode! Because there is no air in space, earthlings need to wear special "pressure suits" or live in the pressurized compartments of the space station.

Radiation   In deep space, there is no atmosphere to give protection from deadly radiation from the sun. On earth, atmospheric gases absorb most of this radiation.

Temperature   A space station needs to withstand great extremes of temperature, depending on how far away it is from the sun. For example, near Mercury the temperature could reach 750°F while in the orbit of Saturn it might drop to -300°F.

Gravity   A space station has to create its own gravity so that the astronauts can lead a more normal life. Living in zero gravity causes bones to become brittle and muscles to waste away. Artificial gravity can be created in a space station by making it rotate at a constant speed. A sensation of gravity will be felt in the outer sections, but there will be zero gravity at the center.

Earth Year 2375

Colonies on Mars Established

Colonization of Mars began in the year A.D. 2375, with 250 volunteers from Island One. Because there was no ozone layer on Mars, the bases were built underground, safe from the dangerous radiation of the sun. Mariner A, the first base built on the southern rim of Mariner Valley, was formed from sealed tunnels covered with rocks and soil. The rocks and soil also helped to insulate the station from the very low temperatures of around -120°F.

Colonists at Mariner A used sunlight (trapped in solar panels) to heat the carbon dioxide that settled overnight in the valley below. The heated carbon dioxide was then used to generate electricity.

These pioneer Martian colonists grew all their own food inside huge domes. Genetically engineered plants from earth grew quite well in the weak sunlight. Warm carbon dioxide pumped in from the generating system heated the domes.

Water was collected every morning from the ice pools at the base of the canyon. The colonists had to be careful not to collect frozen carbon dioxide (dry ice) that evaporated as soon as the temperature reached -95°F. All water was carefully recycled.

The main work of the Martian settlers was to carry out a series of experiments that could lead to the terraforming of planets. (By terraforming a planet, scientists make conditions on the planet more like those on earth — and more suitable for plants and humans.) For many years, low-flying hovercraft carried dark sand and rocks from gravel mines near Mariner A and spread them over the northern icecap. Eventually, this dark sandy material absorbed enough warmth to melt some of the ice, and water began to flow into the nearby canyons where algae and mosses could be planted.

Today, in Earth Year 3970

After centuries of terraforming, colonists can see the results of a gradual climate change. Mars is now more than twenty degrees warmer. The air is still thin, but it has a much higher concentration of oxygen. A very thin ozone layer has begun to form, and Mars is beginning to look much like earth might have looked millions of years ago when plants first began to cover the land.

Earth Year 2783

Colonies on Mercury Established

Three colonies of earthlings from the Armstrong Base were settled on this very hostile planet between Earth Year 2783 and Earth Year 2896. One group formed a settlement at Caloris 1. They were trained to extract the planet's valuable nickel, tantalum, and magnesium ores, using solar and electric furnaces. At Caloris 2, other colonists specialized in the production of high-temperature glass from meteor fragments. Caloris 3 colonists were specialists in maintaining power supplies to all the Caloris settlements and servicing the huge mirrors used in solar furnaces.

The Caloris colonists all lived deep under the ground in metal tunnels to avoid the extreme range of temperatures and intense ultraviolet radiation. All that could be seen aboveground were the mirrors, used for power generation; the solar furnaces; and the radar-controlled early warning meteor destroyer system.

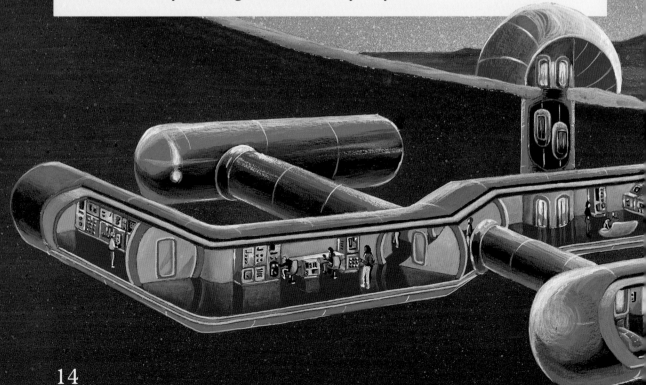

Today, in Earth Year 3970

The Caloris metalworkers operate in shifts, focusing the mirrors of their solar furnaces onto large crucibles containing tantalum and magnesium ores. The high temperatures melt the ores, and the molten metal runs into pipes below the ground. Here it is rolled into sheets before being transported to other colonies and used in the assembly of spacecraft and starships.

For the workers on Mercury, each day lasts about eight Earth weeks. Above the Caloris colonies, the fierce sun shines for about twenty Earth days continuously. While the sun is overhead, it is far too hot for the colonists to be outside. The surface temperature can reach 788°F, and the ultraviolet radiation is very intense.

It is possible to move around on the surface of Mercury only during evening and dawn, because during the nights the temperatures drop to -240°F. So it is at evening and dawn that the teams of glassworkers from Caloris scavenge the surface of Mercury for meteorite debris that can be used to make a special shatterproof glass. This material is collected and stored so that it can be melted down and reshaped in the solar furnaces.

During the long and very cold nights (which last about four Earth weeks) metalworkers at Caloris 1 take time off for recreation and study.

Earth Year 2956

Work Begins on Venus — the Hostile Planet

In Earth Year 1966, the Russian unmanned space probe *Venera 3* landed on Venus and was very quickly crushed by the tremendous atmospheric pressure (which is about ninety times greater than that on earth). But later, technologically advanced space probes successfully gathered data about the thick yellow clouds of sulfuric acid and carbon dioxide that covered the planet's surface, creating a powerful greenhouse effect. From the data, scientists knew that temperatures on the ground reached about 900°F. Violent electrical storms endangered visiting spacecraft and made radio communication impossible.

Nearly a thousand years later, in Earth Year 2956, scientists from Island One and Armstrong began a terraforming project to change the atmosphere on Venus. The idea was to "seed" the surface of the planet with blue-green algae that would slowly convert the carbon dioxide into oxygen. The oxygen released by the algae would reflect more of the sun's rays, cooling the atmosphere and reducing the planet's greenhouse effect. The atmospheric pressure would also fall as the dense clouds of carbon dioxide were gradually absorbed by the algae.

The first stage in the terraforming project was to get some water onto the planet's surface so that algae could grow. But how could this be done when the surface temperature was well above the boiling point of water? The solution was for astro-engineers to capture ice asteroids orbiting beyond Mars and deflect them with rockets to Venus. Over many years, hundreds of ice asteroids were sent crashing to the surface of Venus. Each one formed great clouds of water vapor that reflected sunlight away from the planet.

By Earth Year 3269, it was thought that the atmosphere on Venus had cooled sufficiently for high-temperature algae to grow.

Today, in Earth Year 3970

The terraforming project on Venus (begun 1014 years ago) has been very successful so far. Rain is now falling over much of the planet, and the maximum temperature is about 127°F. Atmospheric pressure is also down. Plans are being made to establish a small colony in the highland region of Beta Regio, with the possibility of using thermal energy from the nearby volcanoes.

Earth Year 3117

Establishment of a Base on Ganymede

By about Earth Year 3105, the communities on Earth, Mars, and Mercury and at Armstrong were needing more hydrogen to fuel nuclear-fusion power systems and spacecraft. Because Jupiter was the largest source of hydrogen, the Interplanetary Council decided to set up a base on Ganymede (one of Jupiter's moons) to collect liquid hydrogen from Jupiter's outer atmosphere.

Over the next twelve years, engineers at Island One built a fleet of special long-distance spacecraft, powered by hydrogen-thermal engines. About eight hundred people set out on the two-year journey to Ganymede. Once they arrived, the colonists built an underground base called Huxley and began collecting Jupiter's hydrogen. Four huge tankers went with the fleet, carrying building materials and power generators for the colony. These hydrotankers returned to Island One and Armstrong with much-needed hydrogen, after a round trip of 900 million miles — a trip that took them about four years.

Ganymede: Site of the Huxley Settlement

Ganymede is one of Jupiter's sixteen moons. It circles Jupiter at a distance of 640,000 miles. Its icy crust is pockmarked by many craters and valleys that have been created by a bombardment of meteorites throughout the years.

Today, in Earth Year 3970

Huxley has now grown to a settlement of 12,500 people. There is a large observatory with both optical and radio telescopes for studying nearby stars. There is no atmosphere on Ganymede, so the sky is always black, and the stars are very clear.

19

Earth Year 3340

Establishment of a Base on Titan

In Earth Year 3340, research teams from bases at Armstrong and Island One set out to explore the five largest moons of Saturn—Titan, Rhea, Iapetus, Dione, and Tethys.

The Titan explorers took with them algae and fungi that could survive in a cold nitrogen/methane atmosphere. These plants would provide all their food. They also hoped to produce oxygen from several other plant species that could grow in the weak sunlight and low temperatures.

The Galileo Base on Titan was built as a special base for scientific research. The exploration teams set up a well-equipped observatory, where astronomers studied the very distant outer planets, Uranus, Neptune, and Pluto. Exploration teams also continued to search for mineral resources on other moons around Saturn and to record changes in the pattern of ice particles that orbit the planet in huge rings.

Titan: Site of the Galileo Base

Titan is Saturn's biggest moon. It is the second biggest moon in the solar system (after Ganymede), with a diameter of 3,080 miles. Surface temperature under its thick layers of gaseous clouds is recorded at -207°F. Winter on Titan lasts for seven and one-half months.

Today, in Earth Year 3970

It is now 630 years since the small colony was started, and now 3,500 scientists and their families live and work on Titan. Plant breeders at Galileo have successfully grown many varieties of delicious fungi and algae. The fungi now grow in the open, extracting all the nutrients they need from methane and rocks near the base. But the algae have been more of a problem — so far they can only be grown inside the glass domes of the colony, where they are used to recycle carbon dioxide and liquid wastes.

Solar energy is too weak to run any generators on Titan, but engineers are using geothermal energy from the moon's rocky interior to drive electrical systems and keep the living quarters warm. Steam from these deep bores also keeps the laboratories and living areas heated.

Valuable information is still being gathered by the research teams at Titan about the planets of Uranus, Neptune, and Pluto. These outer planets, however, have not been colonized by earthlings to date.

Earth Year 3891

New Planets Discovered

In Earth Year 3891, the Titan observatory sent reports to the Interplanetary Council on earth about some astonishing discoveries. For many years, Titan scientists had been observing Alpha Centauri, one of the star systems nearest earth's solar system. The sensors at the Titan observatory had actually recorded faint images of planets orbiting this bright three-star system. The observatory had also received puzzling radio signals from the region. These signals suggested that some form of intelligent life existed on planets near Alpha Centauri.

By Earth Year 3895, the Interplanetary Council made plans for a long and dangerous mission to explore the distant Alpha Centauri system. Such a mission was possible because of radical new designs in engine technology.

Earth Year 3933

Starship *Daedalus* Is Launched: Destination Alpha Centauri

Scientists were very excited by the reports of planets in the Alpha Centauri system and the possibility of finding other life forms.

Conventional nuclear-thermal engines, which had a top speed of about 24,000 miles per hour, would have taken 1,026,496,800 (over a billion) years to reach Alpha Centauri! However, discoveries of high-temperature metal alloys and improvements in rocket engine technology made deep space travel possible.

In Earth Year 3872, engineers on the Deep Space Technology Program at Armstrong had designed a hydrogen-fusion rocket engine capable of speeds close to 80,000,000 miles per hour. This was the engine to power the *Daedalus* starship built at Island One.

Finally, in Earth Year 3933, *Daedalus* was launched from Island One on its long and dangerous mission to Alpha Centauri. This huge starship carried 380 people on a voyage that was scheduled to take at least thirty-seven years. Many of the men and women on board would never return to the solar system. *Daedalus* and its crew would explore and then colonize any suitable planets in the Alpha Centauri system. Children born on *Daedalus* would be trained to bring the ship back to the earth network after nearly a century of travel and exploration among distant planets.

Journey to Alpha Centauri

Inside *Daedalus*, the astronauts settled down to an active routine of survival and maintenance. No one had ever traveled beyond the solar system before, and no spacecraft had ever moved at such a speed.

After the starship had swung through the orbit of Jupiter, the crew aimed it at its target—the distant star system Alpha Centauri, twenty-five trillion miles away.

The propulsion chamber on *Daedalus* is made of special cerium and tantalum alloys to withstand the powerful nuclear fusion explosions that push it along at a top speed of about 80,000,000 miles per hour.

The upper deck is used for growing plant food. The air supply is boosted with oxygen given off by the plants, and all water and liquid waste is recycled and purified before it is used again by the plants and people.

A fully equipped observatory monitors radiation levels, comet movements, and star positions. All information is transmitted to Armstrong Base.

Computers control most of the navigation, but constant checks have to be made with the large computers at Armstrong and on earth.

Fifty girls and twenty-eight boys were chosen as part of this mission. They were all about eight to twelve years old when they left Island One. More children will be born on the starship during the journey to replace those adults that die. All will be educated in space technology while on board.

Five small landing craft are carried outside *Daedalus* to be used for low-level exploration and for landing astronauts on the planets surrounding Alpha Centauri.

Earth Year 3970

Discovery of Icarus

This Interplanetary Council's report finishes with the exciting news that important messages have just been received from starship *Daedalus*. The starship is now orbiting a planet in the Alpha Centauri system that looks very similar to earth. There appear to be water and clouds, as well as volcanic activity in several places.

The microwave signals telling of the discovery of a new planet have taken over four years to reach our base at Armstrong, so we don't know what discoveries have been made since they were sent. At the moment we have some wonderful computer images of the very bright star system that we call Alpha Centauri. We also have some very good images of three orbiting planets. Messages from the crew of *Daedalus* inform us that preparations are being made to send out landing craft to one of these planets. The crew has named the planet Icarus.

All earthlings on our solar system bases have been informed, and we now wait for more signals to come from the space explorers on *Daedalus*.

PART TWO

Facts about the Planets

The Solar System

Earth (home of the earthlings) is just one small planet in a vast neighborhood that is bigger than any neighborhood you can imagine. This neighborhood is made up of a star (the sun) and its family of planets and their moons.

Planet	Distance from Sun
Mercury	34,700,000 miles
Venus	64,900,000 miles
Earth	93,000,000 miles
Mars	136,800,000 miles
Jupiter	467,000,000 miles
Saturn	856,000,000 miles
Uranus	1,720,000,000 miles
Neptune	2,698,000,000 miles
Pluto	3,500,000,000 miles

Pluto

Mercury

The planet closest to the sun, with an extreme range of temperatures.

Diameter — 2,930 miles, slightly larger than our moon.

Gravity — A 110-pound person on Earth would weigh just 42 pounds on Mercury.

Atmosphere — None. The sky would seem black. Extreme radiation.

Temperature — Highest, 810°F (hot enough to melt lead); lowest, -290°F.

Moons — None.

Surface — Dust and rock. Surface pitted with many meteor craters. Largest crater, the Caloris Basin, is 780 miles across.

Distance from Sun — 34,700,000 miles.

Sunlight — About six times brighter than on Earth. Extreme ultraviolet radiation hazard due to lack of ozone layer.

Rotation — Gravitational pull of the sun slows Mercury's rate of spin. One rotation = 59 Earth days.

Orbit around Sun — One Mercury year = 88 Earth days. (Mercury is very close to the sun. If it didn't orbit the sun so quickly, it could get dragged into the sun and destroyed.)

31

Venus

The hottest and most inhospitable of all planets.

Diameter   7,300 miles (almost the same size as Earth).

Gravity   A 110-pound person on Earth would weigh 101 pounds on Venus.

Atmosphere   Mostly carbon dioxide (97%), which traps heat from the sun. Some water vapor (2%). Yellow clouds of sulfuric acid hide the surface. No oxygen. Violent electrical storms are almost continuous and make Venus a very hostile planet.

Temperatures   At cloud tops, 55°F; at ground surface, 900°F (hot enough to melt lead or zinc), caused by greenhouse gases in the atmosphere.

Moons   None.

Surface   Dry rocky plains and mountain ranges. At least two massive volcanoes.

Distance from Sun   64,900,000 miles.

Sunlight   Thick clouds of sulfuric acid prevent sunlight from reaching surface except at poles, where it would be 1.6 times brighter than on Earth.

Rotation   Venus rotates very slowly in the opposite direction of Earth, so the sun rises in the west and sets in the east. One Venus day = 243 Earth days.

Orbit around Sun   One Venus year = 225 Earth days.

Earth

The only planet known to have liquid water and to support life.

Diameter   7,654 miles.

Atmosphere   Water vapor and a mixture of gases — 78% nitrogen, 21% oxygen, 0.9% argon, and carbon dioxide — provide a mild greenhouse effect, keeping the planet warm enough to support life. Ozone layer prevents ultraviolet radiation damage to plants and animals.

Temperatures   Highest, 134°F (Libya); lowest, -129°F (Antarctica).

Moons   One.

Surface   Land and rocks 29%; water 71%. Many active volcanoes and some meteor craters. Only planet in the solar system with surface water.

Distance from Sun 93,000,000 miles.

Sunlight   Equivalent to being about 2 inches from a 75-watt light.

Rotation   Once every 23 hours and 56 minutes.

Orbit around Sun   One year = 365 days.

35

Mars

A cold, dry planet about half the size of the earth.

Diameter

4,072 miles.

Gravity

A 110-pound person on Earth would weigh 42 pounds on Mars.

Atmosphere

Seems to have "lost" most of its gases at some time in the past. Present atmosphere too thin to protect life from deadly ultraviolet radiation. Mostly carbon dioxide (95%), with some nitrogen (2.7%) and traces of oxygen and other gases. Small amounts of water vapor form fog and clouds near the surface.

Temperatures

Highest, -24°F; lowest, -191°F.

Moons

Two — Deimos and Phobos.

Surface

Mostly rocks and dusty sand stained red by iron oxides. Frozen carbon dioxide and water (ice) in polar regions. Many meteor craters mark the surface. A giant extinct volcano, Olympus Mons, is twice the height of Mt. Everest. A huge canyon, known as the Mariner Valley, runs 3,000 miles long and up to 140 miles wide.

Distance from Sun

136,800,000 miles.

Sunlight

About half as bright as on Earth.

Rotation

Almost the same as Earth: 24 hours and 37 minutes.

Orbit around Sun

One Mars year = 687 Earth days.

Jupiter

Bigger and heavier than all the other planets and moons put together.

Diameter 85,700 miles.

Gravity Twice that of Earth. A 110-pound person on Earth would weigh 257 pounds on Jupiter.

Atmosphere Clouds of ammonium hydrosulphide, ice crystals, and water drops circulate over a huge mass of liquid hydrogen that forms this planet. Constant electrical storms and lightning.

Temperature At cloud tops, -200°F; near the center, probably 54,000°F.

Moons Sixteen. The four largest moons are Ganymede, Callisto, Io, and Europa.

Surface Hydrogen gas.

Distance from Sun 467,000,000 miles.

Sunlight The sun's intensity would be 1/27 the brightness that we see on Earth. Full sunlight would be equivalent to being about 10 inches from a 75-watt light.

Rotation One Jupiter day = 10 hours.

Orbit around Sun One Jupiter year = 11.9 Earth years.

39

Saturn

The second-largest planet in the solar system.

Diameter

72,400 miles.

Gravity

Almost the same as that on Earth.
A 110-pound person on Earth would weigh
118 pounds on Saturn.

Atmosphere

Mostly hydrogen, with some helium.

Temperature

At cloud tops, -300°F; at core, probably
54,000°F.

Moons

Rings of ice particles and a total of twenty-
three orbiting moons. The largest moon, Titan,
is larger than Mercury and slightly smaller
than Mars. It is one of the few moons in the
solar system known to have an atmosphere—
mostly nitrogen (just like the earth) with small
amounts of methane.

Surface

Hydrogen and helium.

Distance from Sun

856,000,000 miles.

Sunlight

Less than 1/90 the brightness we see on Earth.
Full sunlight would be the same as being
about 3 feet from a 75-watt light.

Rotation

One Saturn day = 10 hours.

Orbit around Sun

One Saturn year = 29.46 Earth years.

41

Uranus

A planet of frozen gases, more than four times the diameter of Earth.

Diameter   30,800 miles.

Gravity   About the same as Earth's. A 110-pound person on Earth would weigh 95 pounds on Uranus.

Atmosphere   Frozen hydrogen, helium, and methane.

Temperature   At cloud tops, -300°F; at center, unknown.

Moons   Several dark rings of rock debris and fifteen known moons—the largest are Oberon, Titania, Umbriel, Ariel, and Miranda.

Surface   Little is known about the surface of Uranus.

Distance from Sun   1,720,000,000 miles.

Sunlight   About 1/360 the brightness we see on Earth. Full sunlight would be the same as being about 6½ feet from a 75-watt light.

Rotation   One Uranus day = 17 hours.

Orbit around Sun   One Uranus year = 84 Earth years.

Neptune

A planet of frozen gases around a core of ice and rock.

Diameter

29,500 miles.

Gravity

About the same as on Earth. A 110-pound person on Earth would weigh 125 pounds on Neptune.

Atmosphere

Frozen hydrogen, methane, and probably helium.

Temperature

At cloud tops, -300°F; at center, unknown.

Moons

Four major rings. Eight known moons; biggest one is Triton.

Surface

Little is known about the surface of Neptune.

Distance from Sun

2,698,000,000 miles.

Sunlight

About 1/900 the brightness on Earth. Full sunlight would be the same as being about 10 feet from a 75-watt light.

Rotation

One Neptune day = 16 hours.

Orbit around Sun

One Neptune year = 165 Earth years.

Pluto

A small rock-and-ice planet about one quarter the size of Earth.

Diameter	1,400 miles. Slightly smaller than the earth's moon.
Gravity	A 110-pound person on Earth would weigh about 4 pounds on Pluto.
Atmosphere	None. Unlike the large "gas" planets, Pluto seems to be mostly frozen methane covering a hard rocky core.
Temperature	About -380°F. The coldest planet.
Moons	One known moon, Charon (700 miles diameter).
Surface	Little is known about the surface of Pluto.
Distance from Sun	3,500,000,000 miles.
Sunlight	About 1/1560 the brightness on Earth. Full sunlight would be the same as being about 13 feet from a 75-watt light.
Rotation	One Pluto day = 6 Earth days.
Orbit around Sun	One Pluto year = 248 Earth years.

Glossary

Acid rain Rain containing pollutants.

Alloy A material made up of two or more metals.

Atmosphere The gases that surround a planet, star, or moon.

Atmospheric pressure The pressure exerted by the atmosphere — the *weight* of the atmosphere.

Cerium A type of metal.

Gamma rays Electromagnetic radiation rays.

Genetic engineering Deliberate alteration of the features of animals or plants by transferring genes from one organism to another.

Geothermal energy Energy from heat produced in the interior of a planet.

Gravity The force of a planet that pulls everything toward its center.

Greenhouse effect The trapping of the sun's warmth in earth's lower atmosphere.

Methane A colorless, odorless part of natural gas.

Nuclear fusion The joining of atomic nuclei to release energy.

Ozone layer Layer of ozone (a form of oxygen) in the upper atmosphere that absorbs ultraviolet radiation.

Sulfuric acid A colorless, dense, corrosive liquid made from the gas sulfur dioxide.

Tantalum A hard grayish-white metallic element used to increase the "hardness" in alloys.

Ultraviolet radiation Energy emitted in the form of electromagnetic waves, with a wavelength shorter than light and longer than X rays.